Today's Superst★rs

Entertainment

Tyra Banks

by Susan K. Mitchell

Gareth Stevens
Publishing

Please visit our web site at: www.garethstevens.com
For a free color catalog describing Gareth Stevens Publishing's
list of high-quality books, call 1-800-542-2595 (USA) or
1-800-387-3178 (Canada).

Library of Congress Cataloging-in-Publication Data

Mitchell, Susan K.
  Tyra Banks / by Susan K. Mitchell.
    p. cm. — (Today's superstars. Entertainment)
  Includes bibliographical references and index.
  ISBN: 978-0-8368-8196-7 (lib. bdg.)
   1. Banks, Tyra. 2. African American models—Biography.   3. Models
  (Person)—United States—Biography.   4. African American actresses—Biography.
  5. African Americans in television broadcasting—Biography.   I. Title.
  HD6073.M772U558   2008
  746.9'2092—dc22
  [B]   2007002997

This edition first published in 2008 by
Gareth Stevens Publishing
A Weekly Reader® Company
1 Reader's Digest Road
Pleasantville, NY 10670-7000 USA

Copyright © 2008 by Gareth Stevens, Inc.

Editor: Gini Holland
Art direction and design: Tammy West
Picture research: Diane Laska-Swanke

Photo credits: Cover, © Katy Winn/CORBIS; p. 5 © Gregorio Binuya/Everett
Collection; p. 7 © Stephanie Diani/CORBIS; p. 9 © U.S. Air Force/USAF/
WireImage.com; p. 10 © Kevin Mazur/WireImage.com; p. 12 © Jean-Paul
Aussenard/WireImage.com; p. 15 © Kristin Callahan/Everett Collection;
pp. 16, 22, 25 © Ron Galella/WireImage.com; p. 20 © Warner Brothers/courtesy
Everett Collection; p. 21 © Columbia Pictures/courtesy Everett Collection;
p. 26 © Lester Cohen/WireImage.com; p. 27 © Chris Farina/CORBIS;
p. 28 © AP Images

Printed in the United States of America

1 2 3 4 5 6 7 8 9 11 10 09 08 07

Contents

Chapter 1

Hanging Up Her Wings

Tyra Banks walked down the runway. Cameras flashed and music blared. She had six-foot long, black wings tied to her shoulders. It was the TV broadcast of the 2005 *Victoria's Secret Fashion Show*. It was also the last time Tyra would work as a model.

It was a perfect end to her modeling career. Tyra was far from finished though. She was beginning a new chapter in her life. "I felt like it was important to walk away while [I was] still on top," said Tyra, "to leave modeling before modeling left me."

Fashion Firsts
Tyra has helped break down some of the barriers for models of color. "When I was

young, I used to see all these models and actresses on the pages of fashion magazines, but none of them were my skin tone," said Tyra. Up until that time, most of the models in magazines were white. Tyra was the first African American model to appear on the cover of many major

American magazines. She was the third African American model with an exclusive deal at a large cosmetics company.

Tyra has tried to change the way African American women are seen in the fashion world. "I think it's still a struggle, and I'm glad I have a large part in breaking those barriers," says Tyra. "I hope and realize that my success . . . is paving the way for other 'firsts' to be achieved until there is no longer a need for the distinction." Tyra's

People magazine put Tyra Banks in their "50 Most Beautiful People" issue twice. In this shot from the 2005 Victoria's Secret Fashion Show, Tyra shows why she makes the list.

Flaws and All

Tyra Banks has cellulite! "I have dimples in the backs of my thighs," she says. "At the Victoria's Secret fashion shows you will never see me walking ... without a little skirt or drape in the back." Being honest about her flaws makes Tyra unique.

She wants girls to know models are not perfect. She often reveals styling tricks that make models look the way they do. "It's irresponsible not to show that stuff," says Tyra. "I want to empower women to embrace their flaws — showing mine is just a part of that."

Tyra gets a lot of fan mail. Many letters are from girls who do not like the way they look. So, Tyra often shows pictures of herself without makeup. "Ninety-nine percent of the modeling industry is fantasy," she says.

wish is that the fashion world will no longer need "firsts" for African American models. She hopes that models of color will one day be completely accepted by the fashion and show business world.

Tyra's Talents

In 2003, Tyra moved to the other side of the runway. Tyra created the TV show *America's Next Top Model*. She wanted a program to show what "really goes into the modeling industry." She

Fact File

In 1997, Tyra received the Michael Award for Supermodel of the Year. The Michael Awards are referred to as the "Oscars" of fashion. The award ceremony helps raise money for the National Children's Leukemia Foundation.

Tyra waits backstage at GMT Studios for the Reality TV show *America's Next Top Model*. Tyra sang the theme song for this show.

also wanted to help young models get their start. "I tell people not to give up on their dream. I had people tell me that I'm 'too black,' not 'black enough'. . . so many things," said Tyra. "All you need is for one person to say yes." That positive attitude — and desire to help others — has taken Tyra a long way from her years as an unknown model.

Chapter 2

A Model Beginning

Tyra Lynne Banks was born on December 4, 1973, in Inglewood, California. She was named Tyra by her grandmother. Tyra's parents, Don and Caroline, both worked full time. Her mother worked as a medical photographer. Her father was a computer consultant. Tyra also has an older brother named Devin.

Tyra grew up in a very close family. Much of her family lived nearby. Family get-togethers happened often. Over time, she grew close to her older brother Devin. "My brother and I have been through it all. We've shared our low points and our successes," said Tyra. "I can't imagine what my life would be like without having him around."

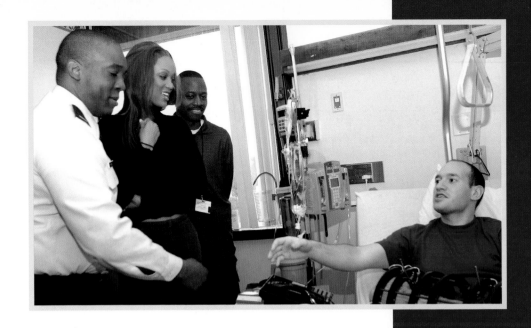

Tyra and her
brother Devin
are close now,
but she says he
was terrible to
her when they
were little. Here,
Devin (*left*) and
Tyra visit a
soldier at
Walter Reed Army
Medical Center.

Tyra was very close to her parents. She
was spoiled by her father. Tyra still calls
herself a "Daddy's Girl." She also looked
up to her mother as a role model.
Unfortunately, her parents got divorced
in 1979. Tyra was only six years old.
Her father moved out but still lived
nearby. Don and Caroline Banks
shared parenting. They always
tried to put their children first.

"I was too young to be hurt, scared, or
upset in any way. As far as I could see, I
had it made. I stayed with Mommy on
the weekdays and with Daddy on the
weekends. I had two birthday parties,
two Christmases. Double the presents,
double the love," recalled Tyra.

Thanks to Ma

Tyra has always been very close to her mother, Caroline. She calls her "Ma." Tyra says her mother taught her many things. She learned about exercise and how to put on makeup from her Ma. Caroline used her skill as a medical photographer to help create Tyra's modeling portfolio. "All the photos in my portfolio for Paris were shot by my mom," said Tyra.

Early in Tyra's career, her mother became her manager. One of the best things she taught Tyra was to keep a level head. "My mother told me to never believe the hype," said Tyra, "but she also told me, 'Don't ever let anyone tell you you can't do something.'"

Tyra's mother (*right*) has appeared on both *America's Next Top Model* and *The Tyra Banks Show* several times.

From Princess to Froggy

When her parents divorced, Tyra was going to a private elementary school. At nine years old, she started to get warts on her hands. Kids at school teased her and called her "Froggy." It was the first time Tyra ever felt bad about herself. She hid her hands in her pockets. She also wore gloves no matter how hot it was outside. Tyra's parents told her that the warts would go away on their own, but they didn't. After much begging and crying, Tyra's father took her to a doctor to have the warts removed. The warts were taken off and never came back. Tyra's self-esteem, however, had been hurt.

The year after Tyra's mother remarried, Tyra entered John Burroughs Middle School. It was a bigger campus than she was used to. She found herself scared and uncomfortable. Two years later, she moved to an all-girl private school called Immaculate Heart Middle and High School. But before she went to this new school, her life took a strange new turn.

Fact File

Tyra and her friends used to go to thrift shops and create outfits. These cost much less than buying new clothes at a store. Tyra's mother also had clothes made for Tyra that looked like popular fashions but cost less.

Hair to Dye For

Tyra had her share of trouble as a teen. Her hair was light, sandy brown as a child. When she was thirteen, she wanted jet black hair like one of her friends. But Tyra's mother said Tyra could not dye her hair until she was sixteen. Tyra sneaked to the beauty salon anyway. Tyra told the hairdresser that her mother gave the okay to get her hair dyed.

Tyra covered up her new black hairdo with a floppy hat that she wore all the way through dinner. Her mother waited until the next morning to bust Tyra. She grounded Tyra for a month. Tyra was not happy to be grounded, but she was happy she finally had really dark hair!

As a teen, Tyra liked to be able to wake up and not worry about her hair, so she liked to wear long, braided hair extensions. Here, in Los Angeles in 1995, she shows how that look works for her.

Body Basics

Before she went to Immaculate Heart, Tyra's body went through big changes. She grew 3 inches (8 centimeters) in three months! By the time she was twelve, Tyra was 5 feet 9 inches (175 cm) tall. She was taller than all of the other students. She was even taller than most of the teachers. She also lost twenty pounds (9 kilograms).

Tyra's family worried that she might have an eating disorder or some other medical problem. Her mother took her to several doctors. They all said Tyra was perfectly healthy.

Tyra heard girls at school say bad things about her. They called her names like "Olive Oyl" or "Lightbulb Head." Soon, Tyra started to feel bad about herself. She spent a lot of time locked in her room. "If there's one period in my life that I don't ever wish to relive, it's puberty," said Tyra. "Before my body went through all these bizarre physical changes, I . . . had lots of friends and was always in trouble for trying to show off and be the class clown."

A New Direction

By the time Tyra was seventeen, her body began to fill out and develop. She felt good about herself again. That same year, a friend, Khefri Riley, told Tyra she should try modeling. Khefri had already signed with a modeling agency. She begged Tyra to give it a try. In 1989, Tyra finally agreed. She started to look for an agency. It was not as easy as Tyra thought it would be.

Everywhere she went, Tyra was turned down. One agent said she looked too "ethnic." Another said they "already had a black woman and didn't want another." She finally found a modeling agent who would give her a chance.

Fact File

As a teen, Tyra tried crazy ways to gain weight. She made chocolate and peanut butter milk shakes before bedtime. She also ate a lot of fattening foods. Nothing worked.

What's So Super?

A supermodel is a model who is successful in many areas. There are many models in the world of fashion. Only a few have become "super." Supermodels are not only famous models, they are smart businesswomen. Many have their own perfume lines. Some have their own brand of clothing. Others have success in TV or films.

Iman was one of the first African American supermodels. She was born and raised in Somalia, Africa. She began modeling in the 1970s and eventually became a U.S. citizen. Her career lasted more than fourteen years. Iman worked with some of the best fashion designers and photographers in the world. She has been in many movies and TV shows. When she stopped modeling, Iman started her own cosmetics company for women of color.

Iman arrives at a benefit for Keep A Child Alive in November 2006. Iman has been married to pop music legend David Bowie since 1992.

Even though she was thin, Tyra grew up in a family that loved food. She said the kitchen was always humming at her house as a child. Here, she shows off her figure at Fall Fashion Week in April 1995.

After looking at Tyra's portfolio, they said they would only use her for runway shows. They said they "didn't feel like the camera liked her face."

Tyra started to get small modeling jobs. She worked hard to balance modeling and school. Tyra loved modeling, but she didn't think it would be her job. She wanted to go to college. When she graduated from high school in 1991, she was accepted to

Loyola Marymount College. She wanted to study film and TV production.

Before Tyra was able to go to college, she got a fantastic opportunity. A French modeling agent offered to send her to Paris, France. She would go for a year to do haute couture fashion shows. It was a chance of a lifetime. Tyra decided to put college on hold. In September 1991, she left for Paris.

On Her Own

For the first time, Tyra was on her own. Paris was exciting, but Tyra was unhappy. She remembers "being lonely in Paris . . . and being extremely homesick with no friends or family around."

In time, Tyra learned to love Paris. She was not into partying with other models. But she learned that she could have fun in other ways. Instead of partying, she went to American movies and bookstores. She went to the city's wonderful museums. She learned to be alone without being lonely. "Paris made me aware of my true

Fact File

Early in her career, Tyra got tired of waiting in line for the "good" makeup artists. So she learned how to put on her own. She is so good that other models often ask her to do their makeup.

Sweet Charity

Tyra loved her years at Immaculate Heart. At first, she was not sure she would like an all-girl school. Eventually, she found good things about a school without boys. "We didn't worry about looking 'cute' to impress guys. We concentrated on our school work and campus events," she said. She learned that girls and women could be strong and be leaders in the world.

In 1992, Tyra created a scholarship to her old high school. "I was privileged to be able to attend such a fine school, led by women who were such good role models," she said. "I established [this scholarship] so that other young women less fortunate than I can have the same opportunity."

inner strengths and helped me hone my survival skills," she said. She was alone, but not for long. The world of French fashion was about to give her a call.

Two weeks after she got to Paris, Tyra was on her first magazine cover. Famous clothing designers began to ask Tyra to model for them. They wanted Tyra to walk in their fashion shows. In one six-day span, she walked down twenty-five runways. It was a rookie modeling record. Tyra Banks was on her way to becoming a model in demand — around the world.

Banking on Success

In 1993, Tyra became the new "fresh face" of Cover Girl cosmetics. She signed an exclusive deal with the company. She was the third African American model to ever do that. It was very important job. Many models had become famous after being "a Cover Girl." Tyra was in magazine ads for the cosmetic company. She also appeared in TV commercials.

That same year, Tyra decided to try acting. She tried out for the role of Jackie Ames on *The Fresh Prince of Bel-Air*. She got the part. Tyra played Will Smith's ex-girlfriend during the fourth season of the show. Her acting talents were praised by critics. Tyra was eager to try more acting.

Tyra appeared in a total of seven episodes of *The Fresh Prince of Bel-Air.* She had scenes with both Alfonso Ribeiro (*left*) and Will Smith (*right*).

Acting Up

Tyra made the leap to the big screen in 1994. She was cast in the movie *Higher Learning*. She played a university student and athlete named Deja. For the film, Tyra had to learn to jump hurdles. As with everything else, she wanted to do her best.

Tyra trained hard with Jeanette Bodin. Ms. Bodin was the head women's

Fact File

Will Smith's real-life wife, Jada Pinkett-Smith, lost the role as his girlfriend on *The Fresh Prince of Bel-Air.* TV producers thought she was too short. Fortunately, Tyra was tall.

A Good Sport

Tyra was a track star in *Higher Learning*, but in real life she is not much of an athlete. As a kid, she tried out for several sports teams. Tyra almost always made it because she was tall. "My coaches saw my five-foot, nine-inch height as an advantage," she said. "That is, until they saw me play." Tyra was very clumsy and uncoordinated. She became the "official benchwarmer."

She might not have much athletic ability, but Tyra loves sports . . . as long as she is watching, not playing! She is a huge basketball fan. She often goes to Los Angeles Lakers games. Tyra has also been a fan of the Women's National Basketball Association (WNBA).

Although she is not the track star she played in *Higher Learning*, Tyra's favorite exercise is a three-mile (5-kilometer) run on the beach. She also loves to dance for exercise.

Modeling sometimes means getting up at three or four o'clock in the morning for a photo shoot. Tyra always insists on getting a full eight hours of sleep each night. Here, she poses at a party for the thirty-third edition of the *Sports Illustrated* Swimsuit Issue in 1996.

college track coach. She also won a gold medal in the 1984 Olympics. Tyra wanted to quit many times, but Jeanette would not let her. Tyra's hard work on the track never made it to the movie. The director ended up using a body double for the hurdle scenes. Tyra was now an actress, but modeling

Fact File

The popular *Sports Illustrated* Swimsuit Issue has been printed for more than thirty years. Being on the cover can raise the amount of money a model gets paid on future modeling jobs.

Commercial Success

Tyra has been in many TV commercials. In 1996, she was in two big commercials during the Super Bowl. Super Bowl commercials are very expensive for companies. They pay millions of dollars for a few seconds on TV. Tyra was in a Pepsi ad with another supermodel, Cindy Crawford. She was also in a Nike commercial with a puppet called Lil' Penny. "Making those spots was really fun," said Tyra.

She was also still making commercials for Cover Girl. In addition to TV, she was in magazine ads. Tyra was part of the very popular "Got Milk?" ads. She was wearing jeans, a white tank-top, and a milk mustache.

was still her main job. In 1996, she was on the cover of the *Sports Illustrated* Swimsuit Issue. She shared the cover with another model. That same year, she was on the cover of *GQ* magazine. She was the first African American woman to be on *GQ*'s cover.

In 1997, Tyra was the first African American woman to be on the cover of the Victoria's Secret catalog. Tyra was on the cover of the *Sports Illustrated* Swimsuit Issue again in 1997. This time she was by herself. "The day it came out, I got on a plane and everybody on the plane knew who I was," Tyra remembers. "It was an overnight change."

Fact File

John Singleton was the director of *Higher Learning*. He and Tyra dated for a few years. Even though they were dating, Tyra still had to try out for a role in his film.

Chapter 5

Bankable Productions

Tyra also became an author, in 1998, with her book, *Tyra's Beauty Inside and Out*. Tyra felt she had to write the book. She said, "People seem to have the idea that I am above the normal human experiences of pain, self-doubt, rejection, and physical imperfections." Showing her flaws and fears helps fans who hope to be like her. In her book, she shares beauty tips. She also talks about loving your looks.

Tyra has starred in many more movies. None of them were big hits, but she always did her best. Some of her best known films are *Coyote Ugly*, *Life Size*, and *Halloween: Resurrection*. Tyra began

Fact File

Tyra has been in several music videos. She has been in videos for Lionel Ritchie, Michael Jackson, George Michael, and Tina Turner.

to realize that TV and film were what she wanted to do full time.

In 2003, she moved to the other side of the camera. She produced two new TV shows. She created the show *America's Next Top Model*. She also created a daily talk show called *The Tyra Banks Show*. She said, "As a kid I knew that I wanted to be a television producer, but I would have never in my wildest dreams imagined that I would have these two amazing shows."

Tyra decided to quit modeling in 2005. Then she turned her full attention to her TV shows. This was one of many smart decisions Tyra has made. She explains, "No matter how famous you are, so much of modeling is waiting for the next job. I [wanted] to be the one who does the hiring, not the one who's waiting to be hired." Now, she is in control.

Tyra has been writing in a journal since she was seven years old. Her journals gave her inspiration for her book. Here, Tyra shows off her book, *Tyra's Beauty Inside and Out.*

Tyra says she likes spending time with kids, like the ones seen here at her TZone youth camp, because they are not impressed with her celebrity status.

In the Zone

Giving to others has always been important to Tyra. In 1999, she opened a camp called TZone. It's for girls thirteen to fifteen years old. Tyra created the camp to inspire leadership and self-esteem in young girls. TZone is near Big Bear Lake in California. Tyra reads every application for camp. "I handpick a diverse group of girls, not only of different cultures but also life experiences and economic backgrounds," she says.

Tyra helps many other charities. Some of her favorite work is with kids. She gives her money, but also her time. Tyra was given the Friendship Award by the Starlight Children's Foundation for her work with kids.

Tyra at the Top

For the future, Tyra's star looks like it will keep rising. Tyra has over fourteen projects in the works. She plans to keep working on her talk show and on *America's Next Top Model*. She is also working on creating a movie with Nickelodeon Films. Tyra wants to be active in TV and films for a very long time. "I'm looking for longevity," she says. Even though Tyra is famous, she still has the same values she was taught as a child. She is often surprised by her success. "I am still amazed when I see a huge crowd of fans show up for an autograph signing, or when photographers jump in my face," says Tyra. "Sometimes I turn around to see who they are waiting for, and when I realize that it's me . . . I have to laugh and shake my head."

Tyra (*left*) hugs others placed with her into the Hard Rock Hall of Fame. In 2007, Tyra auctioned this green blouse and other items on *The Tyra Banks Show* to raise money for TZone.

Fact File

Tyra suffers from a fear of dolphins. Since she was young, she has had bad dreams of them bumping her while she was swimming. She faced her fears on an episode of her talk show.

Undercover with Tyra

Tyra has been an inmate at a women's prison. She has been a male rapper and a 350 pound woman. These are a few of the disguises Tyra has worn on *The Tyra Banks Show*. As a heavy woman, she found most people would not make eye contact with her. "I would . . . smile, but 90 percent of [the people] didn't smile back," she said. She hoped the episode would make people think. Tyra believes making fun of large people is "the last accepted form of discrimination."

Tyra was blasted in the media in 2007 for gaining weight. She fought back on her TV show and in the magazines. Tyra posed in a bathing suit for the cover of *People* magazine to show she was proud of her body, no matter its size. Below, she dances with with Nelly Furtado on *The Tyra Banks Show*.

Time Line

1973	Tyra Lynne Banks is born in Inglewood, California on December 4th.
1991	Travels to Paris for modeling job; walks in record twenty-five shows in six days.
1992	Returns to the United States; forms her own company.
1993	Gets TV role on *The Fresh Prince of Bel-Air*; signs exclusive contract with Cover Girl.
1994	Has a role in the movie *Higher Learning*.
1996	First African American woman on a *GQ* magazine cover.
1997	First African American model on the cover of the *Sports Illustrated* swimsuit issue; becomes first African American model on Victoria's Secret's catalog cover.
1998	Publishes her book *Tyra's Beauty Inside and Out*.
2000	Stars in the TV movie *Life Size* and big screen film *Coyote Ugly*
2003	Creates and produces TV reality series *America's Next Top Model*.
2005	Creates and produces her talk show *The Tyra Banks Show*; retires from modeling.
2007	Bigger but better, she poses in a bikini on the cover of *Shape* magazine.

Glossary

banned — kept from being in a certain place, industry, or publication.

body double — a person who looks like an actor and fills in for the actor during some movie scenes.

critics — people whose jobs are to give their opinions about creative work such as acting.

discrimination — treating a group of people badly because of what they look like or for some other reason, such as religion, gender, or disability.

eating disorder — a medical and psychological problem that causes people to behave in ways that make them lose too much weight.

exclusive — an agreement to work for only one company.

haute couture — French for "high fashion"; clothing from high-end designers.

hype — excessive publicity that usually exaggerates the good qualities of a person or product.

modeling agency — a company that represents models and finds them jobs.

portfolio — a collection of a model's photographs.

runway — the narrow, raised platform on which a model walks.

self-esteem — the way a person feels about herself or himself.

To Find Out More

Books

Tyra Banks. Black Americans of Achievement (series).
  Pam Levin (Chelsea House)

Tyra's Beauty Inside and Out. Tyra Banks with Vanessa
  Thomas Bush (HarperPerennial)

Videos

America's Next Top Model – Cycle 1 (Paramount) NR

Life Size (Walt Disney Video) NR

The Fresh Prince of Bel-Air – The Complete Fourth Season
  (Warner Home Video) NR

Web Sites

America's Next Top Model
http://www.cwtv.com/shows/americas-next-top-model
Photos and clips from Tyra's reality series.

The Tyra Banks Show
http://tyrashow.warnerbros.com/
News and information about Tyra and her talks show.

Tyra Banks
www.tyrabanks.com
Official Web site. Photo galleries and many extras.

Index

About the Author

Susan K. Mitchell has always loved books, movies, and music. She is a teacher and author of several children's picture books. Susan has also written many nonfiction chapter books for kids. She has a wonderful husband, two daughters, a dog, two cats, and an adopted pet squirrel. She dedicates this book to her mother, Robbie . . . the most beautiful woman in the world.